My Keepsake Recipes

A PERSONAL
COLLECTION
OF MEALS,
MEMORIES,
AND
TRADITIONS

PAINTINGS BY
Sandy Lynam Clough

HARVEST HOUSE PUBLISHERS
Eugene, Oregon 97402

My Keepsake Recipes
Copyright © 1996 by Sandy Lynam Clough
Published by Harvest House Publishers
Eugene, Oregon 97402

ISBN 1-56507-494-7

Scripture quotations are from the Holy Bible, New International Version® Copyright ©1973, 1978, 1984 by the International Bible Society. Used by permission of Zondervan Publishing House.

Design and production by Garborg Design Works, Minneapolis, Minnesota.

Harvest House Publishers has made every effort to trace the ownership of all quotes and poems in this book. In the event of any question arising from the use of any quote or poem, we regret any error made and will be pleased to make the necessary correction in future editions of this book.

Printed in the United States of America.

96 97 98 99 00 01 02 03 04 05 /QK/ 10 9 8 7 6 5 4 3 2 1

I can't stuff the aroma of Aunt Susie's apple pie in a kitchen drawer so that I get a whiff each time I reach for a potholder. And even if I painted pictures of Grandma's Christmas cookies all over my kitchen walls and waved gingerbread potpourri in the air, it would still not be a country Christmas morning.

How do I store a memory?

So many times it is the special food itself that brings back memories of friends and family. It could be the casserole from a new friend in a strange city, a congealed salad that was always on the table at Christmas, Mama's cantaloupe ice cream or your best friend's fudge that starts you down memory lane. Maybe you have left a memory of yourself everywhere you took your same "specialty" (the only dish you know how to make well). Favorite foods from friends and family become heirlooms, releasing memories of good times, touching all the senses—the sight, the smell, the touch, the familiar taste, and even the sounds.

And though the food cannot be kept for a reminiscence, the memories it invokes can be safely stored in the recipe. Every time an heirloom recipe is prepared, the sight, the taste, the aroma remind us of people and places we hold dear. They comfort us with the familiar.

How can you store a memory? By keeping your special recipes in this album. By writing your memories of a special meal or attaching a favorite photo. By passing on to your children the taste of home unique to your family.

You can also use this album to encourage a friend to record her keepsake recipes. A new bride could begin her own collection, or her mother or mother-in-law could arm her with secret family recipes that she could then add her own traditions to. Sharing your favorite dishes in <u>My Keepsake Recipes</u> would also make a thoughtful going-away gift for a friend.

This simple book can be a treasury of memories, released in your kitchen each time you open its pages. I hope you'll enjoy it well and use it often.

Sandy Lynam Clough

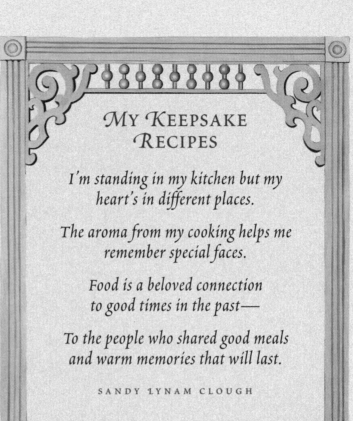

My Keepsake Recipes

*I'm standing in my kitchen but my
heart's in different places.*

*The aroma from my cooking helps me
remember special faces.*

*Food is a beloved connection
to good times in the past—*

*To the people who shared good meals
and warm memories that will last.*

SANDY LYNAM CLOUGH

Treasured Recipes & Traditions of

_____

Stay, stay at home, my heart, and rest;
Home-keeping hearts are happiest.

HENRY WADSWORTH LONGFELLOW

Spread love everywhere you go: first of all in your own house. Give love to your children, to your wife or husband, to a next door neighbor...Let no one ever come to you without leaving better and happier. Be the living expression of God's kindness; kindness in your face, kindness in your eyes, kindness in your smile, kindness in your warm greeting.

MOTHER TERESA

When one has tasted watermelon, he knows what the angels eat.

MARK TWAIN

Offer hospitality to one another.
1 PETER 4:9

The most sacred flame, the fire of domestic love.
HARRIET BEECHER STOWE

Special Holiday Recipes

Sandy Clough

Serve one another in love.

GALATIANS 5:13

INDEX

For home and
happiness and friends,

we give thanks

with all our hearts.